THOUGHTS

ON

POOR-HOUSES,

With a View to their general Reform,

PARTICULARLY THAT OF

SALISBURY,

COMPARING IT WITH THE MORE IMPROVED ONES OF

Shrewſbury, Iſle of Wight, Hull, Boldre, *&c.*

AND DEDUCTIONS DRAWN,

USEFUL TO OTHER POOR-HOUSES.

To which is added, an Account

OF THE

POPULATION OF SALISBURY,

WITH OBSERVATIONS THEREON.

BY HENRY WANSEY, F.A.S.

" A Diſeaſe well known, is half cured."

London:

Printed for T. Cadell, jun. and W. Davies, Strand.

1801.

[*Price Eighteen-pence.*]

J. Easton, Printer,
High-street, Salisbury.

TO THE WORSHIPFUL

THE

MAYOR AND JUSTICES

OF THE

CITY OF NEW SARUM,

AND TO THE

CHURCHWARDENS AND OVERSEERS

Of the three united Parishes of

ST. THOMAS, ST. EDMUND, AND ST. MARTIN.

My fellow Citizens,

THE chief design of addressing the following Observations to you, is, that by stating the Expences of our Poor, it may be contrasted with the Management of the Poor in other places, and thereby furnish useful Hints to some more able persons to digest a proper Plan for relieving them at less expence; for it is a serious and alarming truth, that our Poor-rates

B   amount

amount to more than a guinea a head upon every inhabitant in the city, one with the other; this I believe is hardly to be paralleled in any other city in England.

In former times of old English hospitality, when gentlemen lived on their estates, the poor were supported by alms distributed from their great housekeeping—but these days are past! The poor were likewise helped by the alms of religious houses and monasteries, which latter relief is still known in some country places, by the name of " Monks meat."

In the 43d year of Queen Elizabeth, when the relief of monasteries ceased, an Act of Parliament passed, ordering " that the overseers of every parish, shall " raise by taxation, a sufficient sum of money weekly, " or otherwise, *to purchase a convenient stock of flax,* " *hemp, wool, thread, iron, and other wares, and stuff to* " *to set the poor on work,* and also for necessary relief " of the lame, impotent, old, blind, and such other " among them, being poor, *as are not able to work.*"

On this law are founded our poor-rates; the design of which was, clearly, to relieve only the impotent, helpless poor, and to provide employment for such as are able to work.

Why

Why then are not other methods of employment found for our poor now left to depend only on the staple trade of the city?

If five or six respectable independent persons would unite their labors to improve the system of management, great savings might be made by finding employment of some kind or other, for every able pauper within the house; but the misfortune is, that the house itself is too small and crouded, to allow of any good plan being effected there. An area scarce forty yards by thirty, is a small space to accommodate three hundred and thirty-three persons.

The true end and design of a workhouse, is well defined in the following advertisement, published some time since in a Lancashire newspaper: " To " train up the children of the poor to habits of in- " dustry, religion, and virtue, in order to make them " useful members of society; to furnish employ- " ment for the poor of all ages, and oblige them to " to earn their own support, as far as their strength " and ability will enable them; to prevent idleness, " dissipation, and vice; and to provide a comfort- " able asylum for old age, disease, or infirmity, when " thereby disabled from pursuing their usual occu- " pations."

I have

I have taken some pains to collect books and papers from different parts of the kingdom, for the purpose of throwing light on this subject, and I hope the result may be useful to my fellow citizens.

I remain Gentlemen,

Your most obedient

Humble Servant,

H. WANSEY.

Castle-street, Salisbury,
April 16, 1801.

Thoughts on Poor-Houses,

AS

Applicable to Salisbury.

MUCH has been said of late of the great encrease of our Poor's Rates in this city.—In the year 1787, their whole amount was 2126*l*. and now this year they are 7249*l*. and yet on the present plan they are found to be far insufficient.

Though it is evident to every thinking person, that something ought and must be done to improve and œconomise the vast sums raised for maintaining the Poor, particularly in improving the management of our Workhouse; yet no public meeting is called, nor any steps taken to remedy many growing evils.

The Overseers, I am convinced, have done all that can reasonably be required of them; but they want more assistance. In all towns noted for the good management of the Poor, there are other officers appointed, such as Guardians, Directors, or Governors; and till we have some regulations of this kind, we are doing but little.

I have taken some pains to collect information respecting that well-regulated House of Industry in the Isle of Wight,

where

where they once laboured under very heavy expences and charges for the maintenance of their Poor, even greater than ourselves.

Their firft ftep, after obtaining an Act of Parliament, was to purchafe a piece of ground, and on it to erect a large commodious houfe, where every convenience might be made, for introducing various kinds of profitable labor, and no perfons who had the ufe of their hands were fuffered to be idle. (They have formed a very extenfive garden attached to the premifes, where they raife as many vegetables as poffible.)

They borrowed 20,000l. for this purpofe.—A narrow mind would have fuppofed this would have increafed their burdens; for the very intereft of this large fum, even at four per cent. would add 800l. a year to their expences.

Quite the contrary; they have reduced the poor-rates from 4s. 3d. per head per week to 1s. 10d. and 2s. In the year 1799, they had paid off 8000l. of the money, and were in a way to difcharge the remainder.

The average number of Poor in their houfe was five hundred in the year 1799, and the amount of their rates 5657l. 4s. 4d. befides a balance in hand of 606l. 3s. 7d. from the former year.

Out of this fum they laid afide 400l. as a building fund; they paid intereft of money 488l. more; they paid falaries to a chaplain, furgeon, governor, matron, fecretary, manufacturer, and fchoolmafter, amounting to 344l. 10s. and had a balance in hand at the end of the year of 206l. 9s. 8d.

The

The average number of our Poor for that same year was two hundred and twenty-three; our poor-rates amounted to near 4000*l.* including some balances paid. There were no salaries paid either to a chaplain, matron, secretary, manufacturer, or schoolmaster, nor money to pay for interest, and yet there was only 154*l.* 4*s.* 9*d.*½ remaining in hand at the end of the year.

Let us next compare together the different modes of feeding and managing the Poor in each house, (and in this statement I refer to the printed account published by each) that we may trace out the causes of the vast difference between their expences.

Salisbury Workhouse.				*Isle of Wight House of Industry.*	
Average of poor in 1798-9 223.				Average of poor in 1798-9 - 500.	
	£.	s.			£. s.
Sums received in all	4361	11		Sums received in all	6644 18
				Deduct laid by for a building fund 400 0	
				Paid interest on 12,200*l.* - 488 0 } 1094 9	
Deduct balance left at the end of the year - - -	154	4		Balance left at the end of the year 206 9	
Clear expenditure	4207	7		Clear expenditure - .5550 .9	

Should have cost	£.	£.		£.
£. 233		393	Meat	516
310		535	Bread	689
106		183 {	Cheese	134
		{	Salt Butter	100
		152 {	Coals	217
		{	Wood Fuel	50
73		217	Malt and Hops	163
		none {	Peas	59
93		few {	Potatoes	62 }
		none {	Rice	55 } 286
		none }	Treacle	30 }
		22	Vegetables	} produced at home
		18	Milk	}
67		175	Grocery	43 soap and candles
			Chandlery	106 other chandlery
		307	Clothing	none

Here

Here we see how the difference arises; for on the left hand margin I have put down the proportion we ought to have consumed, according to the regulations of the Isle of Wight. First, in the article of meat we might have saved 160l.—in bread 225l.—cheese 77l.—malt and hops 144l.—and yet their Poor in that proportion were fed better and more to their content than ours. It will be seen that we have been falling in vegetables, pulse, &c. which form a cheaper and equally salutary food, and more expensive in the dearer articles of consumption. For they, besides the produce of a large garden of six acres, have expended in peas, potatoes, rice, and treacle, 206l. and we have used no more, without a garden, than what cost 22l. In grocery and chandlery we have exceeded the proportion by more than a hundred pounds. In the article of clothing we expended 307l. and they nothing worth mentioning, as they always manufacture what they use within the house, and make it up there. What they manufacture more than they consume, (which is considerable) they sell and make a profit on. This forms a separate account, and the profit reduces the clothing expence to very little. Further, —they bought in as much leather as cost them (240l., all which was made up into shoes within the house.

At the end of the year they had used in the house, of their own making, four hundred and six ells of sheeting, worth 1s. 8d. or 1s. 9d. the ell; three hundred and two yards of dowlas, worth 1s. 6d. the ell; and eight hundred and four yards of other linen cloth; nine hundred and fifty-seven yards of lincy, besides mops, yarn, shoe thread, &c.; besides which, they had in store twenty-six loads of farmers' and millers' sacks, biscuit bags, and charcoal bags, worth 20l. and twice as much in value more of lincy, linen, and woollen cloth,

besides

besides a thousand pounds weight of thread, worth 50*l.* and many other useful articles, which it would be tedious to mention. But this is sufficient to shew what great things may be done, when a proper system of management is adopted.

I shall next state the cost * of our own Poor for a few years past, and contrast it with the cost of other houses of the kind, at the same period, and their different modes of management, as best to be adopted for our practice.

In the year 1770, the city procured an Act of Parliament, to consolidate the poor-rates of the three parishes; at that time the rates amounted to 1500*l.* only; now they are 7249*l.* The Out-Poor then cost 241*l.* 14*s.* 6*d.*; now 2436*l.*; and next year the amount will be much more, if some effectual regulations are not adopted.

The whole expence is borne at this time by eight hundred and seventy-eight housekeepers (out of one thousand three hundred and fifty-three, the rest being excused through poverty); the expence averages at 8*l.* per house.

* Besides the assistance of our poor-rates, a considerable sum was raised last winter by subscription, to deliver hot pork, and pea-soup to the Poor, at their dinner hour, three, and sometimes four days in the week. It was conducted much to the approbation of the principal inhabitants, many of whom attended and tasted it, and had messes sent to their houses.

A quart of this and a bit of pork, a poor man could not have provided for himself at less expence than sixpence; it was sold at three-halfpence, and the quantity delivered this season, was twenty-two thousand two hundred quarts, and as many pieces of pork with them.

Observations from the printed Report of the State of the Poor House at Salisbury, and its Receipts and Payments, compared with Shrewsbury.

Average number of Poor in the house for the last three years is two hundred and sixteen, in maintaining of whom the consumption has been

	per ann.				each per ann.				each per week.
	£.	s.	d.		£.	s.	d.		d.
Of Meat -	383	0	0	i. e.	1	15	2	that is	8¼
Cheese -	177	12	0		0	16	5		3¾
Bread -	529	6	0		2	10	0		11¼
Fuel -	122	8	4						2½
Grocery and chandlery	170	9	0		1	0	0		4¼
Milk & vegetables	40	0	0						
Malt & hops on average of 4 years	229	11	8		1	1	3		5

Clothing 182*l.* or 16*s.* 9*d.* per head per annum.

Medical expences from 40 to 50*l.* per annum.

N.B. In the year 1795, the article of bread cost 706*l.* 5*s.* 6*d.* and exclusive of that and meat, there was paid for other provisions 475*l.*, such as cheese, grocery, vegetables, and milk, which is near 100*l.* more than the above average.

Earnings in the house on an average of four years, are 556*l.* 19*s.* 2*d.* or 10*l.* 15*s.* per week, not quite 1*s.* per week per head. Expences of maintaining them is from 3*s.* 6*d.* to 4*s.* per week per head, besides house-rent, wages, &c.; that is, they at present earn about one-fourth of their living.

Besides

Besides giving a salary to the Master of the house of 25l. per annum, you profess to allow him 10 per cent. on their earnings, but if you deduct the expences attending it, such as sizing, tool hire, premiums to overlookers, &c. which you ought to do, you will find that you have, instead of 10 per cent., given the master 12, and 14 per cent. Building expences have likewise been confiderable:

		£.	s.	d.
In 1797	it was	89	2	$2\frac{1}{2}$
1798	-	184	19	$2\frac{1}{2}$
1799	-	242	0	0
1800	-	139	0	0

And yet, you are so crampt for room that you have not means of employing your Poor, nor any garden* to raise your vegetables, every morsel of which, you are obliged to pay money for, and for want of which conveniency, you cannot make that advantage of a more general use of vegetables, which would with good management much lessen your consumption of meat.

Average number of Poor in Salisbury House in the year 1799, two hundred and sixty-six.

	£.	s.	d.		£.	s.	d.
Amount of rates including balance from former year					4279	16	9
Money borrowed, and not then paid				-	200	0	0
					4479	16	9
Deduct on militia account -	145	0	0				
Balance paid to succeeding overseers	25	2	7				
					170	2	7
					4309	14	2

* This year a small garden has been rented, but not at all adequate to the purpose.

Cost of Articles of Consumption in Salisbury House, 1799.

		£.	s.	d.	£.	s.	d.	d.
					Each per ann.			**Each per week.**
Meat	-	586	0	0	2	4	0	10
Cheese	-	241	0	0	0	18	0	4
Bread	-	1017	0	0	3	16	6	1½
Grocery and chandlery	}	229	2	0	}			
Milk and vegetables	}	83	0	0	} 1	3	3½	
Malt & Hops		367	0	0	1	5	6	6
Law expences		70	0	0				
Coal & Fuel		122	8	0				
Out Poor	-	1115	0	0				

Clothing 393*l*. nearly 30*s*. per head one with the other.

N. B. In provisions alone each person cost 8*l*. 12*s*. 7½*d*. in this year, nothing reckoned for groceries; which, if added, would make their cost for keep only, 4*s*. 5½*d*. per head per week, besides other general expences.

Let us compare it with Shrewsbury House:

Average number of Poor at Shrewsbury in 1799, two hundred and ninety.

Amount of rates including balance of former year	4017	14	0
Deduct interest of money and principal paid off -	821	17	0
	3195	17	0
Balance left to be paid to succeeding overseers -	148	6	0
	3047	11	0

Cost

Cost of Articles of Consumption in Shrewsbury House, 1799.

	£.	s.	d.	Each per ann. £. s. d.			Each per week. d.
Meat -	411	0	0	1	8	4	6½
Cheese, but-ter & milk }	159	0	0	0	11	0	2½
Bread -	592	0	0	2	0	11	9¾
Grocery and chandlery, inclu. tea }	96	0	0				
Vegetables besides a garden }	75	0	0	0	12	0	2¾
Malt & hops	180	18	0	12	6	0	
Law expences	52	0	0				
Coal & fuel for oven }	105	7	0				
Out-poor under	300	0	0				

Clothing—all manufactured and made up in the house, besides felling to the amount of 586l. 13s.

N. B. In provisions each person cost 5l. 4s. per annum, or 2s. per head per week.

By this we see that there is ample room for amending our plan; since at Shrewsbury the cost of the Poor is not much more than half the expence of ours.

We will next consider the different modes of government, adopted in such houses as are celebrated for good management.

Plan of the Government of the Poor in different Parts of the Kingdom.

ISLE OF WIGHT.

An Act of Parliament procured in 1776. A Corporation formed of twenty-four Directors and thirty-six Guardians, (besides the Churchwardens and Overseers to make the poor rates, collect and disburse to the Poor,)—the Guardians are annually chosen at the Vestry Meetings,—the Directors chosen by ballot out of the Guardians,—four quarterly meetings held by all the Directors and Guardians,—fine for the absentees,—any Directors chosen and refusing to serve, to pay 6l. penalty, a Guardian 4l.—qualification, is possessing 50l. per annum in land or houses, or renting 100l.—Fines for non attendance, from 1l. to 5l.

Five Guardians and two Directors to act monthly in rotation.

The effect of these regulations have been, to lower the expences from 4s. 3d. per head per week to 1s. 10d. and 2s.

Inhabitants, thirty thousand.—Poor-rates 5657l.

Average number of Poor in the house five hundred, for the year 1799.

Order of Diet, Isle of Wight.

	Breakfast.	Dinner.	Supper.
Sunday	Bread and butter	Boiled beef	Potatoes
Monday	Barley broth	Peas with beef liquor	Bread and butter
Tuesday	Bread and butter	Mutton broth	Potatoes
Wednesday	Barley broth	Beef or mutton broth	Bread and butter
Thursday	Bread and butter	Rice pudding	Potatoes
Friday	Barley broth	Pork not above 50lb. with potatoes or peas	Potatoes
Saturday	Barley broth	Rice milk	Potatoes or bread & butter

N. B. They have now substituted pork for beef, finding it better and cheaper; the sick have fresh meat and broth, with other provisions, according to the surgeon's directions, who is desired to give written orders for the same.

SHREWSBURY.

An Act of Parliament. Eight Guardians and twelve Directors. The vestries annually elect eight Guardians, out of whom the Directors chuse four to fill up their number, four going out every year. Fines for non attendance. Qualifications are * * * * * The effect has been, to lower the poor-rates one third.

Number of the resident Poor in 1798, was two hundred and seventy-four, who cost 1s. 9d. per head per week, their earnings in one year being 84l.

Inhabitants, nine thousand.—Poor-rates 4000l.

Order

Order of Diet, Shrewsbury.

	Breakfast.	Dinner.	Supper.
Sunday	Broth	Butchers' meat and roots	Broth
Monday	Milk pottage	Bread and cheese	Mashed potatoes
Tuesday	Ditto	Stewed meat with potatoes or other garden stuff	Pea soup
Wednesday	Ditto	Pork stewed and peas pudding	Broth
Thursday	Broth	Butchers' meat and roots	Ditto
Friday	Milk pottage	Yeast dumplings, or hot cakes (1 pound for a man) with milk	Mashed potatoes
Saturday	Ditto	Stewed meat with potatoes or other garden stuff	Broth

Account of a Week's Average Consumption of Provisions, in December, 1798, in Shrewsbury Workhouse; two hundred and seventy-four Persons:

	£.	s.	d.
560lb. meat, at 2½d. per lb.	5	16	8
173lb. flour (from 30 bush. of wheat) at 6s. 8d. per bush.	10	0	0
1710lb. potatoes (18 bushels, at 1s. 3d. per bushel)	1	2	6
134 gal. small beer, at 3d. per gallon	1	13	6
22 gal. ale, at 10d. per gallon	0	18	4
74lb. cheese, at 3½d. per lb.	1	1	7
156 gal. skimmed milk, and 4lb. of butter	1	9	0
Peas, oatmeal, salt, groceries	A	5	0
Not 1s. 8¾d. per head.	23	6	7

Though these articles are much dearer with us, yet this will serve as a general direction to arranging other workhouses.

HULL.

A Governor and twenty-four Guardians. The Mayor, Recorder, and Aldermen, are all Guardians ex officio.

They

They have reduced their poor-rates from 8320*l.* to about half.—Inhabitants, twenty-seven thousand five hundred.

They have three hundred and twenty in the house, and their poor cost 3*s.* 11¼*d.* per head per week.

Their earnings in 1790 amounted to 847*l.*

Account of a Week's Cost of Provisions in Hull Work-house, in March, 1800, after their new Regulations. Their Number three hundred and twenty.

	Left last week		Bought this week		Total received		Left this week		Expended		Price		Total		
	ft.	lb.	ft.	lb.	ft.	lb.	ft.	lb.	ft.	lb.	s.	d.	£	s.	d.
Beef	25	0	35	11	60	11	30	0	30	11	6			15	6
Ox-heads	0	0	0	0	0	0	0	0							0
Mutton	0	0	0	6¼	0	6¼	0	0	0	6¼	0	6	0	3	1½
Bread	168	0	140	13	308	13	134	0	174	13	3	9½	2	9	9
Peas	46 bu.		11 bu.		57 bu.		55 bu.		2 bu.		12	0	1		0
Cheese	149	0	0	0	149	0	137	0			6	7			4
Butter	0	0	0	4	0	4	0	0	0	4	1	4	0	5	2
Candles	0	0	0	14	0	14	0	10	0				0	2	2
Soap	0	13	0	30	0	43	0	33	0	10	7½	0		6	3
Salt	0	0	0	8	0	8	0	5	0	3	3½	0	9	4½	
Potatoes	95 pe.		0	0	95 pe.		81 pe.		14 pe.		8½	0	9	11	
Treacle	3	2	17	12	21	0	14	0	7		5	7½	1	19	4¼
Flour	3	0	15	0	18	0	11	0	7	0	4	3	1	9	9
Beer	72 gal.		108 gal.		180 gal.		72 gal.		108 gal.		3	1	7	0	
Oatmeal	2 bu.		0 bu.		2 bu.		0	0	2 bu.						0
Groceries													3	11	4½
Milk													3	4	7½

		£	s.	d.
		62	17	0¼
Earnings this week	- - - -	5	7	4½
Expended more than earned	-	57	9	8

Of 3*s.* 7*d.* per head per week.

Persons

Perſons in the Houſe, March 8, 1800.

Hired Servants	- - - -	4	
Paupers, Men	- - 61		
Women	- 119	316	320
Children	- 136		
Dead	- - - -	0	
Diſcharged	- - - -	0	
Ran away	- - - -	0	
Received this week	- - -	0	

320 in the Houſe.

nces ~~Earnings~~ per head this week 3*s*. 11¼*d*.—The above method of keeping their weekly accounts is a very good one.

BOLDRE.

Boldre Workhouſe, beſides the Overſeers and Churchwardens, is under the inſpection of twenty-four Guardians, choſen annually from the neighbouring gentlemen, of whom ſix act in rotation every three months. The houſe is new built, on a convenient healthy ſpot, in the midſt of two acres and an half of garden ground, well cultivated for the uſe of the houſe.

The Committee meet on the firſt Thurſday in every month, at the Poor-houſe, at ten o'clock in the forenoon, from Lady-day to Michaelmas, and at eleven, from Michaelmas to Lady-day. Number of reſident poor, forty-ſeven.

They coſt per head per week 1*s*. 8*d*. and their earnings are in four weeks 5*l*. 7*s*. 1½*d*. Forty-ſeven perſons. They ſpin linen and woollen yarn, and weave; and the children knit woollen gloves for exportation. They ſpin and weave moſt of their linen and woollen apparel.

Order

Order of Diet at Boldre.

	Breakfast.	Dinner.	Supper.
Sunday	Milk pottage	Beef, pork, or veal, 4 oz. a man, 3 oz. a child; garden-stuff not limited, having a large garden	Bread and cheese
Monday	Ditto	The remains with vegetables, and bread or cheese to make out	Ditto
Tuesday	Ditto	Rice pudding or dumplings, 1lb. for a man, 3qrs. for a child	Ditto
Wednesday	Ditto	Meat and roots	Ditto
Thursday	Ditto	The remains, and made out with bread and vegetables	Ditto
Friday	Ditto	Meat soup with vegetables and bread	Ditto
Saturday	Ditto	House cleared of all scraps, in soup or broth with bread and potatoes	Ditto

Cost of forty-seven Poor in Boldre, for four weeks, in Oct. 1799.

	£.	s.	d.		s.	d.	
First week cost –	3	17	3½	i. e.	1	7½	per head
Second ditto –	3	19	11½		1	8¼	
Third ditto –	4	0	11½		1	8½	
Fourth ditto –	3	19	11½		1	8¼	
	15	18	2				
Four weeks earnings	5	7	0½				
	10	11	1½	i. e.	1	1½	per head per week

DUBLIN.

In 1797 they reduced by a reform in the management, their expences from 3s. 0¼d. per head per week in one year, to 1s. 11d.

WINTER-

WINTERSLOW.

Order of Diet.

	Breakfast.	Dinner.	Supper.
Sunday	Pottage	Meat broth	Bread and herring
Monday	Ditto	Peas broth	Mashed potatoes
Tuesday	Ditto	Meat broth	Ditto
Wednesday	Ditto	Peas broth	Bread and herring
Thursday	Ditto	Meat broth	Mashed potatoes
Friday	Ditto	Bread and herring	Ditto
Saturday	Ditto	Peas broth	Ditto

Receipt for the meat broth.				*Receipt for the peas broth.*		
lb.		d.		lb.		d.
3 Meat	-	10		4 Peas	-	9
2 Barley	-	$4\frac{1}{2}$		$2\frac{1}{2}$ Barley	-	$5\frac{1}{2}$
10 Potatoes	-	5		10 Potatoes	-	5
4 Bread	-	11		4 Bread	-	11
40 Water	-	———		40 Water	-	———
—		2 $6\frac{1}{2}$		—		2 $6\frac{1}{2}$

59 boiled away to 48, yields
for 32 persons $1\frac{1}{2}$ lb. each.

$60\frac{1}{2}$ boiled away to 48, yields
for 32 persons $1\frac{1}{2}$ lb. each.

N. B. A few onions or leeks boiled separately, and then
thrown in, will much improve it.

BRISTOL.

Plan of the Government of the Poor of the Nineteen United Parishes, in St. Peter's Workhouse.

Incorporated by Act of Parliament. A Governor, Deputy-Governor, Treasurer, and Guardians, besides officers within the house.

		£.
Amount of poor-rates for one year, to March 31, 1800		15437
Rents of lands - 156 5 6		
Balance from former year 2437 9 0		2593
		18030
Left at the end of the year balance in hand -		5339
		12691

Inhabitants in Bristol, about eighty-four thousand.

Average number of persons in the house, three hundred and twenty-two.

	£.	s.	d.
Chaplain's salary -	40	0	0
Schoolmaster's ditto -	50	0	0
Matron's ditto - -	30	0	0
Gratuities to those two	20	10	0
Other Servants & Nurses	146	0	0
Salary to Apothecary	60	0	0 besides 55*l.* for medicines.

Clothing three hundred and twenty-two persons, 255*l.* that is 15*s.* 10*d.* per head, one with the other.

Costs per head per week in provisions of all kinds, 3*s.* 4¾*d.*

Order

Order of Diet at Bristol.

	Breakfast.	Dinner.	Supper.
Monday	Gruel or rice milk	Meat 1lb. each	Bread & cheese
Tuesday	Ditto	Meat broth	Ditto
Wednesday	Ditto	Rice milk	Ditto
Thursday	Ditto	Meat 1lb. each	Ditto
Friday	Ditto	Broth with rice	Ditto
Saturday	Ditto	Salt fish	Ditto
Sunday	Ditto	Bread & cheese	Ditto

They consumed one hundred and forty-eight *Cwt.* of rice, forty-two bushels of peas, and other vegetables, to the amount of 70*l.* besides the produce of their garden.

	£.	s.		£.	s.	d.	
The meat cost	664	0	i. e.	0	0	9¼	per head per week.
Wheat & flour	1237	0		0	1	6	ditto.
Cheese	183	0	}	0	0	3	ditto.
Butter	10	0					
Malt and hops	233	0		0	0	0¾	ditto, or 14*s.* 6*d.* per head per annum.

Poor-rates at Bristol are only about 2*s.* 3*d.* in the pound, that is, houses last year rented at 30*l.* per annum, were assessed at 20*l.* and 3*l.* 6*s.* levied thereon.

FARNHAM.

A new house built about the year 1790, begun under excellent regulations, and many bonds paid off, but for want of an Act of Parliament to enforce the orders and attendance of officers,

officers, with fines, &c. it came to be badly managed, and the poor are now farmed out. A perfon is paid 30*l*. per annum, as a Perpetual Overfeer to affift the other officers, in diftributing relief, &c., who is very induftrious in the bufinefs, and gives fatisfaction.

Number in the houfe on an average laft year, one hundred and twenty-five.—Poor-rates 14*s*. in the pound half rent—the former year only 9*s*.—Number of inhabitants four thoufand.—Expence of feeding and clothing, about 30*l*. a week, or 1560*l*. per annum.—Governed under the regulations of Gilbert's Act.—One Vifitor, one Guardian, Churchwardens, and Overfeers.

Diet.—Hot meat three days in the week.—Potatoes inftead of bread, and broth for breakfaft.—Bread and cheefe for fupper.

Mode of paying the poor out of the houfe weekly, according to the number in family, and their earnings, proportioned to rife and fall of flour and bread in the parifh.

A Schoolmafter to teach the children to read, and who reads Family Prayers to the people, mornings and evenings.

SALISBURY WORKHOUSE.

The Churchwardens and Overfeers are annually elected at Eafter, ferve one year, and go out of office at the end of that period altogether; there are fix Churchwardens, and ten Overfeers.

seers. There is one Master who resides in the Poor-house, but no Governor, Director, or Guardian.

Inhabitants, about seven thousand.—Poor-rates in 1800, 7249*l.*

Order of Diet at Salisbury.

	Breakfast.	Dinner.	Supper.
Monday	Pottage	Bread and cheese	Bread & cheese
Tuesday	Ditto	Ditto	Ditto
Wednesday	Ditto	Ditto	Ditto
Thursday	Ditto	6 oz. of beef, or 4 oz. of bacon, with vegetables	Ditto
Friday	Ditto	Ditto	Ditto
Saturday	Ditto	Bread and cheese	Ditto
Sunday	Ditto	6 oz. of beef, or 4 oz. of bacon, with vegetables	Ditto

Allowance per week to each, seven pounds of bread, and ten ounces of cheese.

Query.— If mashed potatoes, or bread and red herring, might not be substituted at supper, sometimes, instead of bread and cheese, with equal satisfaction, and be a saving; especially if the potatoes were the produce of your garden?

A general

A general Table of useful References for Salisbury.

Years.	Average poor in the house.	Earnings £.	Poor's-rates. £.	Out-Poor. £.	Deaths.	Clothing. £. s.	
1780	169	252	1611	463	27	61	7
1781	219	339	1640	401	19	144	11
1782	194	391	1767	429	33	91	10
1783	194	368	2023	351	16	118	12
1784	180	311	1650	328	44	120	15
1785	172	295	1628	399	24	123	2
1786	212	342	1904	482	25	164	15
1787	189	321	2135	515	15	146	15
1788	206	318	1643	552	23	157	9
1789	197	461	2156	491	12	198	8
1790	200	459	2180	611	13	210	11
1791	199	491	2196	499	16	164	3
1792	188	411	2298	467	15	171	2
1793	199	411	2305	525	11	95	8
1794	199	512	2559	473	24	111	17
1795	204	539	3143	705	20	160	11
1796	206	585	3466	836	15	162	3
1797	221	612	2990	1047	13	221	18
1798	224	497	3199	954	19	276	0
1799	266	587	5511	1115	22	268	10
1800	312	548	7249	2436	20	356	0

$$
\begin{array}{llll}
\text{Anno } 1780, & 27 \text{ died out of} & 169 \\
1781, & 19 & 219 \\
1782, & 33 & 194 \\
1783, & 16 & 194 \\
1784, & 44 & 180 \\
1785, & 24 & 172 \\
1786, & 25 & 212 \\
& \overline{7)188} & \overline{7)1340} \\
& \overline{27} \quad \text{out of} & \overline{191\frac{1}{4}}
\end{array}
$$

The

The health of the poor has been confiderably amended of late, in confequence of putting in ventilators, and white-wafhing every part of the houfe, at leaft twice a year, as the following extract from the above table will fhew; for in the laft year only twenty died out of three hundred and twelve, which is about a fifteenth; whereas, in the average of feven years, from 1780 to 1786, there died twenty-feven out of one hundred and ninety-two, a feventh part, befides a faving of above 30l. in the hofpital account. (In the London Hofpitals of St. Thomas and Bartholomew, a thirteenth part die; and in the Hotel Dieu, at Paris, a fifth of all that are admitted.)

Having now premifed thefe feveral ftatements, for the full elucidation of the fubject, I leave it to the public at large to draw their feveral inferences, as may beft apply to their own views of improvement; fo that with the help of thefe documents, they may form fuch regulations, as they may think the fubject deferves.

The preliminary rule for the management of the poor in the Ifle of Wight Workhoufe, is, that all fingle perfons, or married ones, without families, who apply for relief, fhall have the houfe offered them, and not be fupported out of it by any penfion. In a well-regulated poor-houfe, 2s. 6d. may fupport a perfon a week in ordinary times; whereas, the fame money given to their management, would be all expended the fecond day; the poor being in general fuch bad managers.

At Birmingham a perfon is conftantly employed at a fixed falary, to vifit the out-poor, at their houfes, which prevents much impofition, and faves the town a great deal of money.

It

It is amazing to confider how much a little faving, made in any article upon a large mafs of people amounts to, or the effect of little earnings of a large number when accumulated. In the return made laft week of the population of Salifbury, three hundred and twenty-fix perfons is the number ftated to be in the work-houfe, and fifty-one of them only employed. If a perfon for inftance, had devifed an employment for thofe that were idle at 2*d.* a day, it would have amounted in one year, to 667*l.* and have faved the collection of one book, at leaft,

I come now to confider under diftinct heads, the diet, clothing, productive labor, education, and fuperintendance to Salifbury Workhoufe.

Diet.

The advantages and favings to be made by encreafing the confumption of vegetables (raifed by yourfelves,) rice and pulfe are great beyond calculation—you have occafion for lefs meat, lefs bread and cheefe, lefs beer, which in thefe times are all articles of heavy expence. At Boldre, two-thirds of their diet are vegetables, and they raife all their pork, and bacon, ufing the refufe garden-ftuff, in feeding the pigs—they vary the different kinds of vegetables, fo as always to make a fuffi-cient change of diet, and their poor are uncommonly healthy from it.—There fhould be an acre of ground at leaft culti-vated for every fifty perfons, the poor in the houfe fhould be employed to dig and work in it, in weeding it, and keeping it clean; a very excellent relief after labour, or illnefs, or where a change of air becomes neceffary, and to afthmatic perfons in particular.—I would not allow a fingle weed to grow

grow a week in such a garden, and every spot of earth should be replanted as fast as it was uncropped.

Besides potatoes, cabbages, spinach, carrots, peas, beans, pot herbs, and sallads—I would recommend a large culture of a root of a very nutritive kind, whose virtues and properties do not seem to be sufficiently understood and known in this country.—While I was in America, I was a witness to the prodigious advantages derived from this nutritive succulent root; I mean the parsnip.—It is a good store to use at any time of the year.—In the United States they keep them three or four years together, in large stacks covered over—the frost never hurts them as they do all other vegetables, and if they become dry and withered, boiling restores them, and sheep or cows will always eat the refuse, and which makes the latter encrease their milk.—In these dear times, what a resource would such a stock have been to our poor! The right method of cultivating them, is to sow them in light ground, as early as October, before the frost, and then they have good time to grow—they should not be dug up till the end of the following year, after they have had some frosty weather on them, you will then have them of a large size, and a full crop, equal in profit to any occupation of the land whatever; and then the ground is in excellent order for a crop of potatoes, or cabbage. By a proper attention to the introduction of the diet, here recommended, I will venture to say, you will save more than 300*l.* a year.

Your method adopted of late ▬▬, of buying an ox in the cattle market, and slaughtering it for the use of the house, appears oeconomical from the following statement, which I publish from your poor-book:

To

	£.	s.	d.		£.	s.	d.
To a bullock bought in market	13	0	0	By 26 sc. 15 lb. at 4¾d.	10	11	9
				Hide 83 lb. at 7s. -	1	9	1
				Tallow, 28 lb. -	0	12	10
Killing and cutting up	0	2	6	Liver, lights, head, & tongue	0	8	6
				Belly and heels -	0	4	0
				Bladder and sweetbread	0	0	6
				Heart - -	0	1	4
	13	2	6		13	8	0

Oct. 8, 1800.

N. B. Beef at this time in the market was 7d. per pound.

The present Overseers have also adopted the plan of keeping pigs, which have been found very profitable, having fatted and killed twenty within the last three months; but these are minor savings compared with the foregoing.

The dressing of potatoes and turnips may be varied, so as to make them relish; mashed potatoes, when ordered alone for supper, instead of bread and cheese, in messes from three quarters of a pound, to one pound two ounces each, and to children eight or ten ounces, will save much as a substitute, in these dear times, for bread and cheese.

Half a red herring to each person, or so that the smaller children may have the lesser halves, may likewise be substituted for cheese.

Clothing.

No money ought to go out of a workhouse to purchase clothing; the people should be put to make every article for themselves, whether woollen, linen, cotton, shoes, leather breeches, caps, or any thing else. In this plan you cannot do better than copy the practice in the Isle of Wight—in

their

their houfe, they ufed up as much leather per annum as coft more than 200*l.*, furnifhed the houfe with as much fheeting, dowlas, and other articles before mentioned, as they had occafion for, fold 200*l.* worth, and there remained more than that amount before-hand in ftore, for either fale or ufe; but this more properly comes to be confidered under the article of productive labour; but I cannot help obferving, that this has been a heavy article of expence to you, amounting in the laft feven years to 1560*l.* ! ! !

Productive Labor.

Here is an ample field for inveftigation, and I muft refer you to the voluminous Mr. Wood, and other writers; only obferving that ten lines from practical obfervation is better than many whole pages founded upon fpeculative knowledge; and that which is ftrictly true in theory, is woefully erroneous oftentimes in practice, and perhaps what I fhall fay here, will be fo denominated by many readers.

Firft, When your poor enter the houfe, take account of what trade they have followed, or underftand, with a view of employing them to the beft advantage.

Second, Thofe who have been bred up ignorant of any occupation, put to picking of oakum, fpinning twine, making bafkets, matts, and haffocks, &c.; every old woman ought to be employed in knitting, even when too feeble for active labor. Yarn ftockings and gloves, are always wanted for exportation, and at this occupation, if the whole houfe (three hundred and twenty-fix) earned but 2*d.* a day, it would amount to 847*l.* 12*s.* in a year; for three hundred and twenty-fix two-pences

per

per day, make three hundred and twenty-six shillings per week, and fifty-two times that sum, makes 847*l.* 12*s.*, which is more money than the house has ever yet earned, in any one year since its establishment.

In the city of Bristol they have an institution, where the blind carry on a manufacture, and nearly maintain themselves by their labor; they manufacture baskets of all kinds, from the coarsest sort for panniers, or butter, to the finest work-baskets for ladies use. A house is fitted up for their reception by subscription, in Milk-street. The front is a shop, where the articles are offered for sale, which they manufacture, and behind it is their work-shop. I have seen more than a dozen at work there together, and a man who is lame, reading to them. They appeared chearful and happy, and their bread eat the sweeter and pleasanter, from being the produce of their own labors. I was surprised, I confess, to see such neat and elegant baskets made by persons totally blind. Such an excellent institution, is worthy of imitation in other towns. Their misfortunes have given them a serious religious turn, for they are fond of singing hymns, and they go often in the evenings to the Methodist chapel, which is not far distant. (In Newcastle workhouse there are near forty children and women employed in pin-making.)

A blacksmith's forge should be erected at some remote corner of the premises, where a man might not only do the business of the house, but fill up all his other time with making nails and other articles for sale.

In Salisbury Workhouse, there are many men who are good gardiners, carpenters, shoemakers, tailors, net-workers, and

other

other handy-crafts; work might surely be found for them; a sixth or an eighth of their earnings should be given them to spend as they pleased, to encourage them. The work they should do, would find always a market, at some price or other. No person, as I before observed, should ever be taken into a poor-house, till account was properly taken of what work he was fit for.

Note. If a board or tablet was put up facing the street, with the following inscription, " One or two gardiners to be " let out by the day, or persons to go on errands, at a short " notice ; women to go out to washing, ironing, charing, " weeding, &c. or to work at any employ by the day, on " reasonable terms," it would be likely to produce some employment for them.

I must further observe, that if it was known, that every person that applies to be taken in, *must work*, you would not have so many applicants as you have.

Education of the Children.

This is the most important of all, and in general least attended to. The young children of those who are taken into the house, should have a peculiar share of attention shewn to them; the institution becomes their alma mater—they should never be suffered to converse with the profligate or vicious, from whom they should be separated entirely ; and the first symptoms of depravity should be suitably corrected. An half hour, at least, every day, should be employed in hearing them read, some of the sober elderly matrons should be employed in this occupation; you never need have any large

number

number from their work at a time; but on Sundays, they should be all in their clean clothes together—the master and mistress being also present. Prayers should be performed mornings and evenings, which is never the case now, I find, and a chapter read by the best scholars amongst them in turn —this would stir up an emulation in them, to acquit themselves well—distributions of occasional rewards is better to work on their minds, than severe punishments—but for swearing or lying, personal correction should be inflicted in the presence of them all,—by these means, and habits of industry acquired, they will be rendered fit to return again into the world, from whose frowns they had taken shelter, and be able to maintain themselves without further assistance.

To see to this, and the putting them out to proper trades and situations in life, should be the province of " the Guar- " dians of the Poor."

VISITORS.

The appointing two Visitors weekly, from the tradesmen of the town, I would strongly recommend, as is the practice at your Infirmary; but as it is too much neglected, even there, I would have it enforced, by a fine on both, in case neither attends, twice in the week at least; these Visitors should have authority to walk through the house, and inspect every part of the institution; see the stores—taste the provisions—see that the lodging rooms were clean and healthy— report how many were out of work, &c.—a book should lie open in the audit room, for the Visitors to make their remarks in it, which should be produced every weekly board.

D

When

When I have thus stated all these improvements, I am sensible that there is still a difficulty to overcome, in getting these things properly inforced; the best institutions from this defect often languish.

You must therefore apply for an Act of Parliament, for new and more extensive powers—to purchase a larger and more convenient piece of ground, and thereon build a house proper for the purpose.—You must have other officers than Overseers—such as Directors and Guardians, as in the Isle of Wight; or a Governor and Deputy, as in Bristol; with their powers distinctly defined, &c.

A short History of the Rise of Poor-Rates.

In the year 1389, the situation of the Poor is first noticed on the records of parliament; for in 12th R. II. a statute was made to restrain them from begging alms without the hundred in which they were born, or lived, but in that district they were authorised and privileged to beg.

Anno 1531, (22d H. VIII.) the Justices were impowered to license persons to beg within certain divisions; and it was not till 27th H. VIII. that the hundred, parishes, or towns, in which the Poor lived, were enjoined to sustain their own Poor, so that they might not be obliged to go about begging publicly. The Churchwardens were then ordered to make collections for them on Sundays, after divine service, with boxes from pew to pew, and this is still the practice in places of worship at New York in America, as I have observed.

In 1537, the statute of the 1st Ed. VI. orders houses to be provided for them, and materials procured to set them on work; and the minister, after the Gospel on Sundays, was to exhort the parishioners to a liberal contribution. The 5th and 6th Ed. VI. went a step further, in ordering a collection for their necessities to be made once every year on a certain Sunday, then to take down in writing what every person was willing to contribute weekly for the ensuing year; this was first called a rate, and hence arose the custom of weekly rates, which is still the mode of collection in some country parishes.

The 5th of Eliz. gives a power against any person of known ability refusing to pay towards the poor's-rate, to be cited to appear before the Justices of the Peace; and if he shall still refuse to pay his share of what was deemed reasonable, he was to be committed to prison. At length, the 14th of Eliz. (1572) granted full authority to the Justices to lay on a general assessment on the opulent inhabitants of every town, district, or hundred, and this has continued ever since.

The famous statute of the 43d of Eliz. (Burn says) is only a fuller explanation of the powers and provisions of the former Act of Parliament. It is, however, the great law of the land, to which reference is always had in doubtful cases, by the Judges themselves. The provisions of it are excellent, and cannot well be altered without creating a greater evil than the cure proposed would be good. If, therefore, any formidable inconvenience arises from the provisions of this Act, you must apply to Parliament for special relief.

This statute limits the number of Overseers not to exceed four for any one parish. In the nineteenth edition of Burn,

1800,

1800, vol. iii. p. 349, a cafe is ftated,—There were five Overfeers chofen for the parifh of St. Chad, at Shrewfbury, to which fome objected, and took occafion from this deviation from the ftatute of 43d Eliz. to refufe to pay their poor-rate. In defence of the election, the ftatute of 13th and 14th Ch. II. was pleaded, which empowers Juftices to appoint *two or more* (indefinitively) in townfhips and villages.

The court would not quafh the appointment, in this cafe, nor did they in the cafe of King and Harman; but confirmed them both upon the plea, that if there was an error in form, it was not fo in the fpirit of the law.

With refpect to the time of appointing Overfeers, the 43d of Eliz. orders, that they fhall be chofen at Eafter, or within a month after, and Juftices are punifhable for neglect of duty in not appointing *any* within that time—penalty 5*l.* But this Act does not fay (in the opinion of fome) they fhall appoint then *only*, and at no other time.

In appointing an Overfeer at any other time, it appears to me, you are liable to an action upon the 43d Eliz.; but in all cafes of this kind, fuch actions are always quafhed in court, upon the plea of " *communis error facit jus.*"

An application to Parliament, in my opinion, will be neceffary, for the reafons I have before ftated (page 34); and I hope it will not be deemed impertinent, if I here fubjoin the Outline of fuch a Bill, as I think would beft anfwer the purpofe:

Outline of a Petition to Parliament, for granting a New Act.

An Act to enlarge the Act made in the 10th of his present Majesty, and to obtain new and more extensive powers—to be granted to certain Trustees, called Directors, Guardians, or Governors, who shall from time to time, have power to make such bye-laws within certain limitations, as may be necessary for the due government of the Poor within the house, appointed for their reception—They shall have power to appoint a Chaplain or Schoolmaster, Matron, or any other officer they may consider necessary within the house (subject to the approbation of (   )—power also to elect a person with a salary, to act as a Perpetual Overseer, who shall visit and relieve the pensionary Poor at their own houses, and be obliged to visit all Paupers' houses at least once in each month; likewise attend at every Friday's Committee to report any thing amiss;—a fixed gratuity over and above his salary may be given at the end of the year —qualifications for Directors and Guardians to be stated— four quarterly meetings of all the Directors, Guardians, and Overseers—fines for non-attendance without reasonable excuse, to be determined by (   )

The Guardians to be chosen at each vestry, four for St. Thomas, four for St. Edmund, and two for St. Martin, and these at a general meeting, to choose three Directors, who are to continue two years, acting in rotation. Half of the ten Guardians, that is, two, two, and one—to be annually chosen in the room of the same number going out of office, and to be elected at Midsummer—powers to be defined.

A Trea-

A Treasurer to be chosen by the Directors and Guardians jointly—all sums of money above a certain amount to be paid by an order on him.

Two Visitors to be appointed from among the tradesmen of the City, one or other, or both of whom, shall visit twice at least, in the week. They shall inspect the health, and condition of the people, taste the provisions, &c. and enter their report of the same, or suggest any improvement they think proper, in a book laid open for them on a table, in the Committee room—a small fine appointed on both, when neither have attended once at least in the week,—to be nominated monthly, (or weekly.) The Directors and Guardians may divide themselves into monthly Committees, so as to act in rotation—Two or more Directors may call a general meeting —They may borrow money for general purposes, (under certain regulations,) for purchasing lands, and building a new and more convenient poor-house; for payment of which, the poor-rates shall become security till discharged, at interest, not exceeding four and a half per cent.; part of the principal to be paid off annually, at least equal to the same amount as the interest, (if not raised by a scheme of survivorship.) The Poor Children to be under the sole government of the Guardians, or whom they may appoint as far as relates to the putting them out apprentice, or to service; they shall see that they are clean, and decently dressed; they shall appoint an Instructor, or Schoolmaster, who shall at certain hours have them come to him, to be instructed to read, and he shall make one of them read a chapter, before he himself reads prayers, which he shall not omit to do every morning and evening, under a penalty of 2s. 6d. each time omitted.

The

The Directors and Guardians, or Churchwardens and Overseers, may let out persons from the house to work on the roads, or at harvest—for scavengers, or to go on messages, or work in a garden, or any other employment they may be fit for, upon receiving a note from any gentleman or tradesman of the town, directed to the Master of the house— They shall appoint rewards to the industrious Poor, and punishment for those who are lazy, filthy, or that swear, or talk obscenely; likewise they shall assist in framing, or suggesting bye-laws, for the better regulation of the house—They shall appoint annual gratuities to the Master, Matron, Inspector, or other officers within the house, at the end of each year, as they shall see proper, or with-hold the same, when in their judgment not merited; it shall be always, however, the same fixed and certain sum.

Churchwardens and Overseers to attend and make the poor-rates as before, and be liable to the laws of the land in every respect, (except that half be chosen at Easter, and half at Michaelmas,) with fines, however, for non-attendance without a reasonable excuse; to be judged of and levied by those Overseers and Churchwardens who are present.

All fines recovered to go in aid of the poor-rates.

POST-

POSTSCRIPT.

In Addition to the Account, (page 29) I beg Leave to state the following Fact :

About four months ago, an exorbitant price was demanded at Lymington-market, by the butchers for their meat. The gentlemen of the neighbourhood met, and determined to send to Salisbury fortnight's beast-market, and buy two heifers on their own account. They did so; and after taking the best pieces of beef for themselves, at the market price of 8*d.* per pound, they sold the remainder to the Poor, at 4½*d.* per pound, and found a profit of three guineas left.

A general spirit of monopoly prevails too much at this time in the country, and as there is no existing law to reach the evil, it must depend on the exertions of generous individuals to counteract this growing pest of society.

ACCOUNT

OF THE

POPULATION OF SALISBURY,

With Observations thereon.

━━━━◆━━━━

In the year 1695, a census was taken, and there were found in

St. Thomas's parish	2665 persons
St. Edmund's	2742
St. Martin's	1569
	6976 total

On an average of seven years, of which 1695 was the middle year, the baptisms were 209—deaths 181—marriages 52.

In the year 1775, the Corporation ordered another account to be taken by their officers, distinguishing those who were strangers; who reported as follow:

Of natives	5334
Strangers, inmates, and servants	692
Totally strangers	709
Doubtful	50
On certificate	71
	6856 total

On an average of seven years, of which 1775 was the middle period, the baptisms were 174—deaths 208—marriages 76.

In

In March, 1801, by order of Government, another cenfus was taken, when it appeared that there were in

	Perfons.	Families.	Inhab. houfes.	Void houfes.
St. Thomas's parifh	2349	482	398	20
St. Edmund's -	2869	788	588	20
St. Martin's -	1749	487	367	12
	6967	1757	1353	52

On an average of the laft feven years, ending 1801, the regifters of the veftries, including Diffenters, give the

	Baptifms	deaths	marriages
Baptifms -	202	deaths 215	marriages 74
The year 1800 alone	203	188	49
In 1793 -	208	272*	82

* The higheft of any year for twenty years.

If this enumeration, when compared with the events, it would be fair to reckon one hundred inhabitants more, for thirty-one houfes adjoining the city, in Caftle-ftreet, Winchefter-ftreet, Milford-hill, and near St. Martin's church; which, though belonging to Milford, are moftly regiftered in Salifbury. There is a very great falling off in the marriages, in the year 1800.

In the year 1782, the number of houses in Salisbury and its environs, were accurately taken by a gentleman of this city:

Houses.

99 from the Alms houses, Exeter-street, to Rook's corner.

74 from Milford-st. corner, to Pale-head.

47 round the Market-place.

158 top of Castle-st. thro' the Cheese-cross, to the Poultry-cross.

58 in High-street.

13 in St. Thomas's Church-yard.

94 from the College (Mr. Wyndham's) to Payne's-hill.

141 from Church-st. hatch, thro' Gigant-st. to St. Anne's-st.

111 from Bedwin-row, thro' Rolleston-st. Brown-st. & Black-friars

88 from Scot's-lane, through Bedwin-row, to the College, east.

69 from Castle-st. thro' Chipper-lane, to Green-croft.

34 from High-st. along the Canal, to corner of Catharine-st.

50 High-st. thro' Silver-st. Butcher-row, includ. st. to Fisherton br.

81 from the corner of Queen-st. to Milford-hill.

86 Three Swans corner, to end of Winchester-st. and road.

93 from the Bell corner, Exeter-st. to St. Martin's church.

128 from Payne's-hill, to the Workhouse in Crane-street.

1424* at 5 to a house, amounts to 7120 persons.

50 more houses at least in courts and alleys.

70 in the Close.

50 in Harnham.

168 in Fisherton.

1762 at 5 to a house, amounts to 8810 persons.

* A decrease in the number of houses in eighteen years, seventy-one. This is accounted for by the erection of large breweries and manufactories, from taking down the old Guild-hall, formerly surrounded with houses, and some houses in St. Thomas's church-yard. Many families now, especially amongst the Poor, live together in one house.

Note,—Our highest population for a century past, appears from 1775 to 1784; it continued nearly the same for ten years after, since which it has declined.

It

It is remarkable, that there has been only one houfe, on a new fite, added for many years. Salifbury has now fewer houfes and inhabitants, than it had one hundred years ago. Its origin was remarkable; in becoming a city within ten years after it began building: for in 1227, King Henry III. (in a charter then granted) ftyles it " his city of New Sarif-" bury." In 1301, it was fortified with a vallum and foffe, two-thirds of which remained within memory of the writer; and to this day there are only forty houfes added without this ancient limit; thirty-one of which belong to Milford parifh.

In the year 1795, a fubfcription was entered into to relieve the Poor by the diftribution of bread:

In St. Martin's parifh 344 applied for 1260 i. e. 3⅔ to a family
St. Thomas's - 143 533 3¼ ditto
St. Edmund's - 468 1610 3½ ditto

955 for 3403 total 3 9/16

In May 1800, bread being 2s. 10d. per gallon, a fubfcription was made to allow the Poor 1s. towards the purchafe of every gallon loaf; likewife a fupply of rice at half price—the applicants then were as follow:

St. Martin's parifh 230 for * 1135 perfons.
St. Thomas's - 161 577 ditto.
St. Edmund's - 543 1336 ditto.

934 for 3048 or 3¼ to a family.

* It accounts for the excefs in St. Martin's parifh, that fome applied for two or three families.

A respectable and worthy Magistrate of the Neighbourhood, having seen this Treatise while under Hand, sent me the following Statement from the Register of his Parish, with his Observations:

WINTERSLOW.

	Bap.	Bur.	Mar.			
10 years to 1780 inclu. }	250	132	47 aver. 5	excefs of bap. more than bur. }	118
				encreafe yearly	$11\frac{8}{10}$
10 years to 1790 inclu. }	208	153	57 aver. 6	excefs of baptifms, ditto. }	55
				encreafe yearly	$5\frac{5}{10}$
10 years to 1800 inclu. }	229	156	35 aver. $3\frac{1}{2}$	excefs of baptifms, ditto. }	73
				encreafe yearly	$7\frac{3}{4}$
total	687	441	139		

Excefs of baptifms in thirty years, two hundred and forty-fix—each year, nearly eight.

Inhabitants, fix hundred and ninety-four.—Houfes, one hundred and forty.

Observations.—What a great falling off in the marriages, in the laft ten years! From 1781 to 1790, the marriages were a quarter more than in the preceding decade, which may account for the encreafe of births in the next decade—but on looking back, cannot account for the excefs of births in the firft decade, on the fame principle.

To

To compare with the foregoing, I have added the fame ſtate-
ments with reſpeĉt to Saliſbury:

	Bap.	Bur.	Mar.				
10 years to 1780	1704	2279	753	aver. 75	exceſs of burials	575	
					yearly decreaſe	57	
10 years to 1790	1982	2232	814	aver. 81	exceſs of burials	250	
					yearly decreaſe	25	
10 years to 1800	2040	2167	763	aver. 76	exceſs of burials	127	
					yearly decreaſe	13	
total	5727	6678	2330				

Exceſs of burials in thirty years, nine hundred and fifty-
two—each year nearly thirty-two.

In the firſt decade, the baptiſms at Winterflow exceed the
deaths, much more than the deaths at Saliſbury exceed the
baptiſms, but in both places the differences leſſen in the next
two decades.

It is to be obſerved, that the deaths in 1771, were very
great (three hundred and four,) on account of a bad ſmall-
pox in the town—for in five years following it, the deaths
were under two hundred, after which it returned to an
average of two hundred and forty-one the next twelve years;
in 1789, it fell again to one hundred and ninety, for four
years; then mounted to the former pitch.

In the return from North Tidworth laſt week, it appears
on a ſeries of fourteen years, there were ninety-ſix births, to
fifty-five burials, with fifteen marriages. This argues it
either a very healthy place, or that there were great emi-
grations.

Population of St. Edmund's Parish.

In 1695, the inhabitants of this parish were 2742.
1801, encreased to   -   -   -   2869.

	Bap.	Mar.	Bur.
From 1692 to 1800—108 years	7686	3272	11172
Average - - - -	71	30	103
Average of the first 36 years -	83⅓	27⅓	92
Second ditto - - - -	61	31¼	106⅓
Third ditto - - - -	69	32⅓	112

	Bap.	Mar.	Bur.
Average of the first 7 years	82	20	84
100 years after - -	81	30	111

St. Thomas's Parish.

In 1695, the inhabitants were 2665 persons.
1801, decreased to 2349.

	Bap.	Mar.	Bur.
In 36 years, to 1727 inclusive	2249	640	1298
Ditto, - 1763 - -	1716	610	1433
Ditto, - 1799 - -	1736	652	1146
Average of first 7 years -	67	15	37
Ditto, 100 years after -	50	18	37

Dr. Price calculates, that

In great cities the deaths are from $\frac{1}{19}$ to $\frac{1}{24}$

In moderate country towns from $\frac{1}{24}$ to $\frac{1}{28}$ and $\frac{1}{30}$

In country villages from $\frac{1}{30}$ to $\frac{1}{50}$ or $\frac{1}{60}$

That in London there dies 1 in 20¾; at Madeira 1 in 50; at Edinburgh 1 in 20⅘; and at Stoke Dameram only 1 in 54; which he therefore pronounces one of the most healthy places he met with. In Salisbury there died 1 in 33½, on an average of the laſt ten years. In country pariſhes the births always exceed the burials, whereas in London there are twenty-ſix burials to eighteen births, or nearly three deaths to two births. On an average of the laſt thirty-ſix years, in Saliſbury there have been two hundred and nineteen burials to one hundred and eighty-four baptiſms, or nearly five deaths to four births, and ſeventy-ſix marriages per annum. But in thirty-ſix years from 1691 to 1727, there were only one hundred and eighty-nine burials to one hundred and ninety-ſix baptiſms, with marriages ſixty-two; including Diſſenters.

Eden's *Eſtimate* (juſt publiſhed) reckons the baptiſms throughout the kingdom, to the burials, as 10 to $8\frac{1}{5}$, and the baptiſms to the population, as 1 to $31\frac{1}{2}$ (p. 28.) but in another page, as 1 to $27\frac{3}{4}$. In Saliſbury, the baptiſms are to the burials, as 10 to $9\frac{1}{4}$, and the baptiſms to the population, as 1 to $35\frac{3}{4}$.

The reſult of the whole is, that the Population of Saliſbury would decline faſt, were it not for new ſettlers; ſince the deaths encreaſe, while the births and marriages decreaſe. But the regiſters are not a ſure criterion alone. Many, to ſave the fee, omit to regiſter, and the Quakers do not baptize. There are many circumſtances continually occurring, ſuch as a briſk trade, which invites new ſettlers; or the contrary, to ſend them away; or ſometimes epidemic diſorders; ſo that no average of years will entirely govern them.

F I N I S.

ERRATA.

Page 17, laſt line, for 3s. 7d. read 3s.

18, l. 11, for *earnings*, read *expences*.

26, l. 4, for *following*, read *foregoing*.

J. Eaſton, Printer,
High‑ſtreet, Saliſbury.

BY THE SAME AUTHOR.

------◆------

Lately publiſhed, price two Shillings,

A NEW EDITION OF

PRACTICAL OBSERVATIONS

ON

WOOL,

AND THE

WOOLLEN MANUFACTURE.

www.ingramcontent.com/pod-product-compliance
Lightning Source LLC
Chambersburg PA
CBHW081724270326
41933CB00017B/3296